EACH DAY, EACH NIGHT

Each Day, Each Night

A daily prayer companion

PAUL SHEPPY
for the
Joint Liturgical Group

CANTERBURY
PRESS
Norwich

© 1997 The Joint Liturgical Group
First published in 1997 by The Canterbury Press Norwich
(a publishing imprint of Hymns Ancient & Modern Limited,
a registered charity)
St Mary's Works, St Mary's Plain
Norwich, Norfolk, NR3 3BH

The Joint Liturgical Group has asserted its right under the
Copyright, Designs and Patents Act, 1988, to be identified
as the Author of this Work

British Library Cataloguing in Publication Data

A catalogue record for this book is available from the British Library

ISBN 1–85311–156–2

*Typeset by David Gregson Associates, Beccles, Suffolk
Printed and bound in Great Britain by St Edmundsbury Press Ltd,
Bury St Edmunds, Suffolk*

Contents

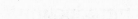

Introduction

This guide is offered to those who are learning to pray, and to those who would like to pray but who find prayer is often squeezed out by the hurry of their daily life.

Even finding prayer hard is good news for those who want to pray, since it shows that they are trying and still believe in its importance.

Why pray?
Prayer was what gave Jesus his link with God, and prayer enables us to look at our daily life in the presence of God. We offer what we will do and what we have done for correction and for blessing. Prayer reminds us that we do not live by bread alone. There is more to life than what we can touch and see, more than we can weigh and measure. We live in dependence upon God, who speaks to us.

So prayer is not just our talk with God, it is also God's talk with us. In this way, like Jesus, we keep in touch with the source of all our life, and we learn to see the world in new and creative ways. We draw on God and find the resources for sharing in a purpose for the world beyond human selfishness. In the encounter with God we are changed and we are drawn step by step into unity with all creation and with God.

What happens when we pray?
Prayer is more than wishful thinking, it is more than hoping against hope. When we pray we are not using 'a slot-machine in the sky'. We begin by letting God speak to us. A word of scripture introduces the prayers in this book, and starts us off in silent listening. We allow ourselves to be challenged or encouraged; we glimpse the glory of God, we rediscover the wonder

of love. We direct our thoughts and minds to God, so that when we come to ask for blessings for others and things for ourselves, we may have begun to see the world and ourselves more as God does.

Sometimes this silence seems empty. If we try to fill the silence too quickly with our words, we will lose the opportunity to hear the voice of God, which is often very quiet, very still. We need to overcome our fear of silence; it is often the opportunity we need to clear a space for God. Then we can bring our days to God, allowing scripture to speak to us and allowing quiet reflection to give us a fresh perspective. It is in the stillness that we find God, not in the rush. While we hurry from one anxiety to another, all we see are the difficulties. When we stop and take our bearings, God draws near and walks with us towards and through our future.

Using this book
The prayers and readings in this selection are designed for those who feel they have little time; but nevertheless they should not be rushed. They are organized in such a way that those who miss a few days can start again—simply by remembering what day of the month it is.

The morning prayers encourage us to worship, to taste and see that God is good. As we experience God's holiness and love, we are made whole ourselves and can begin to live creative and fruitful lives.

In the evening, the mood is more reflective. We offer our achievements and failures to God, so that what has been good may be made perfect and what has been bad may be purged. As we wait for God and with God, we receive pardon and hope, and we find the rest and peace which God alone can give.

As well as the daily round of prayer through the month, Christians celebrate particular days and times which we call

Feasts and Seasons. If you would like to share in this you can do so by turning to the section of Special Feasts and Seasons.

We start with Sunday prayers. These are specially provided for those who cannot get to church, for whatever reason. Special prayers are also provided for Advent, for Christmas, for Epiphany, for Lent, for the four days of Maundy Thursday, Good Friday, Holy Saturday and Easter Sunday, and for Pentecost.

Each of the feasts and seasons marks in a special way the ministry of Jesus, born of Mary, living our life, dying our death, leading us to new life, offering us God's energy, and inviting us to share in the work of God's kingdom. If you want to use the prayers for Advent and Lent, one way of doing so is just to use the special seasonal prayers once a week—on Fridays, perhaps. For the rest of the week you can just use the ordinary daily series.

The prayers and meditations in this book are written to help you start and end the day with God. As you use them, do not let what is on the page be a prison. The words are only signposts to point us to God. If you find your mind being drawn on, do not stop just because the page does. Go on with God. You are praying as you walk beyond the signpost towards the goal.

Going on in prayer
This book is designed to help you start on your journey. It offers you a simple way to keep in touch day by day; and when you forget, it gives you a direct means of picking up again. There is more to praying than there is in this small book, but the longest journey has to begin somewhere, and the end is reached one step at a time.

A last word
This book is designed to fit into a pocket or bag, so that you can use it on the bus, on the train, in a crowded café, on a park

bench—anywhere. Wherever your desert is, make an oasis; renew your life with God.

If prayer is a new experience for you, develop a regular habit. Each day, each night, make a time and a place to do what Jesus did as he kept in touch with the source of life itself—God, who is our beginning, our purpose, our way, our end.

The Lord's Prayer—A Modern Version

Our Father in heaven,
hallowed be your name,
your kingdom come,
your will be done,
on earth as in heaven.
Give us today our daily bread.
Forgive us our sins
as we forgive those who sin against us.
Save us from the time of trial
and deliver us from evil.
For the kingdom, the power, and the glory
    are yours
now and for ever. Amen.

The Lord's Prayer—A Traditional Version

Our Father, who art in heaven,
hallowed be thy name,
thy kingdom come,
thy will be done,
on earth as it is in heaven.
Give us this day our daily bread;
and forgive us our trespasses,
as we forgive those who trespass against us;
and lead us not into temptation,
but deliver us from evil.
For thine is the kingdom,
the power, and the glory,
for ever and ever. Amen.

The Thirty-One Days

Day 1 ✳ *Morning*

This is the day that the Lord has made; let us rejoice and be glad in it.
Psalm 118:24

SCRIPTURE
You shall go out in joy, and be led back in peace; the mountains and the hills before you shall burst into song, and all the trees of the field shall clap their hands.
Isaiah 55:12

MEDITATION
The keynote of my life in God is joy. This joy is not simply my own personal delight, but the song of the whole creation. Today I will look for opportunities to rejoice rather than to complain, to fix my attention on love rather than on self. I will look for God in the ordinary and the predictable as well as in the unusual and unexpected.

Remain still and silent for a moment, so that God may speak to you. As you think about what may happen today, listen to the challenge that comes to you to rejoice.

PRAYER FOR TODAY
Loving God, teach me how to rejoice in all that occurs today. When I am crossed, teach me about the cross of Jesus. When I am encouraged, grant me the grace of humility. When you meet me in my friend and in my enemy, fill me with love. So fill me with your joy, that I may be a source of joy for others; through Jesus Christ our Lord.

THE LORD'S PRAYER

Day 1 ☽ *Evening*

It is you who light my lamp; the Lord, my God, lights up my darkness.   *Psalm 18:28*

Take time to be quiet at the end of the day, to review it before God. Offer it all to God—the good and the bad—and take the opportunity to learn how to live the gospel more completely tomorrow.

SCRIPTURE
'See, I have taken your guilt away from you, and I will clothe you with festal apparel.'   *Zechariah 3:4b*

MEDITATION
If I turn from the sin of my past, God will not allow it to be my continual accuser. There is a future for me, which is still joy. I cannot avoid the consequences of my failings, but I need not be a failure. God needs the broken-hearted, not the big-headed.

PRAYER
Loving God, not all of today has been my best for you. Forgive me not only for the wrong I have done, but for my self-satisfaction when things have gone well. Speak your forgiveness to me—the word that makes me new. Grant me the grace to let go of those hurts, imagined and real, which I have received today; through Jesus Christ our Lord.

A LAST PRAYER
Send rest, O Lord, to all whom I have met today. Grant strength to those whose day is now beginning.

Day 2 ✳ Morning

I will bless the Lord at all times; his praise shall continually be in my mouth.   *Psalm 34:1*

SCRIPTURE

Whatever is true, whatever is honourable, whatever is just, whatever is pure, whatever is pleasing, whatever is commendable, if there is any excellence and if there is anything worthy of praise, think about these things.   *Philippians 4:8*

MEDITATION

As I begin this day I offer it and myself to God to be filled with what is good and pure, so that I may be transfigured in my relationships and dealings with others. I am a temple of the Holy Spirit, and as I live today I will allow God to live through me for the well-being of others.

In silence think of those whom you know you will meet today, and those whom you will meet unexpectedly. Greet them in this silence in a way which fulfils St Paul's words to us.

PRAYER FOR TODAY

Holy God, defend me today from all that would harm love for others and for you. Keep me from meanness of spirit, from hardness of heart, from sharpness of tongue. Give me the grace to serve you in my neighbour and in the stranger readily and cheerfully, always looking for what is good and true; through Jesus Christ our Lord.

THE LORD'S PRAYER

Day 2 ◐ *Evening*

If I say, 'Surely the darkness shall cover me, and the light
around me become night,' even the darkness is not dark to you;
the night is as bright as the day, for darkness is as light to you.

Psalm 139:11, 12

*As the day draws to its close, allow the light of God to shine in
the darkness. In the darkness of failure, seek the light of God's
forgiveness. Place your confidence in God's mercy and love
which reach into our despair.*

SCRIPTURE
Thus says the Lord God, the Holy One of Israel. In returning
and rest you shall be saved; in quietness and in trust shall be
your strength.   *Isaiah 30:15*

MEDITATION
The darkness which threatens to overwhelm me is as light to
God! Since my life is hidden in God, I am safe. The darkness
will never master the light. I can come home at last—at the end
of this day—to God, who transforms me by love. And not just
me, but the whole creation.

PRAYER
Eternal God, you dwell in light, and so much of my life is dark.
Shine in my darkness that I may not only see myself truly, but
may also behold you. Renew me and restore me; teach me how
to live aright; through Jesus Christ our Lord.

A LAST PRAYER
As the night falls, give me untroubled sleep that I may rise
refreshed to serve you. Be present wherever darkness over-
shadows your creation, and grant your people everywhere to be
a light for the world.

Day 3 ✳ *Morning*

Clap your hands, all you peoples; shout to God with loud songs
of joy.   *Psalm 47:1*

SCRIPTURE
Go your way, eat the fat and drink sweet wine and send portions
of them to those for whom nothing is prepared, for this day is
holy to our Lord; and do not be grieved, for the joy of the Lord
is your strength.   *Nehemiah 8:10*

MEDITATION
I can delight in the holiness of God! The gifts of creation are for
me to enjoy in the company of others. I am enriched not so
much by what I can hold on to, but by what I give away. Today
I will share what I have with those I so often ignore.

*In silence before God, remember those whom you are inclined
to refuse, those whom you think undeserving. Here is your
opportunity to discover the joy which is God's strength. Today
you can learn how that strength comes to full flower in your
weakness.*

PRAYER FOR TODAY
Joyful God, you have showered so much upon me. Help me to
see in the outstretched hand of the beggar, in the loneliness of
the house-bound, in the tense face of the anxious, the opportunity to spread before them a banquet for their joy and strength;
through Jesus Christ our Lord.

THE LORD'S PRAYER

Day 3 ● *Evening*

Create in me a clean heart, O God, and put a new and right spirit within me.

Psalm 51:10

In silent prayer remember all that has happened today. If there are events which arise to accuse you, turn to God for cleansing and renewal. Beyond forgiveness for what is done, there is the possibility of a conversion of mind and heart which will open a future otherwise closed.

SCRIPTURE

I will be a wall of fire round about, and I will be the glory within.

Zechariah 2:5

MEDITATION

God is my place of protection and my source of hope. The prophet saw the city of Jerusalem as a refuge for the people of his day, where God's presence might blaze among them. Now in the company of all Christian people I can be shielded and beautified by the fire of God which refines and purges me.

PRAYER

God of the fire within and around me, purify me as the smith refines silver and gold, that I may be fashioned to display your glory in the world. Be a wall of fire around those in danger, and be the glory of those whose life is set in hardship; through Jesus Christ our Lord.

A LAST PRAYER

Grant to me sleep that is a friend, give rest to those who lie awake, guard those who work this night, and on your world bestow the gift of peace.

Day 4 ❈ *Morning*

The earth is the Lord's and all that is in it, the world, and those who live in it.   *Psalm 24:1*

SCRIPTURE
Blessed are those who hunger and thirst for righteousness, for they will be filled … Blessed are the peacemakers, for they will be called the children of God.   *Matthew 5:6, 9*

MEDITATION
Jesus turns our values upside down. If I want to be full, I must be hungry—how extraordinary! Today I will make justice and peace my guiding rule in all I do or say. I will look out and not in, to the needs of others rather than to my own wants. I will find Christ in the helpless and hopeless.

In the quietness with God remember those with whom you are cross. Find an opportunity today to make peace with them, even if you know you are in the right. Do right, and leave the rest to God.

PRAYER FOR TODAY
God of justice and peace, it is so easy to be in the right and to lose friends. Teach me to leave my rights behind in following you, so that the hungry may be satisfied and the broken healed; through Jesus Christ our Lord.

THE LORD'S PRAYER

Day 4 ☽ Evening

As the eyes of servants look to the hand of their master, as the eyes of a maid to the hand of her mistress, so our eyes look to the Lord our God, until he has mercy upon us.

Psalm 123:2

Perhaps throughout this day you have been busy about many things, and now you have the opportunity to stop and rest awhile. Now is the time for that one thing which you truly need, the companionship of Jesus in which you learn about yourself and about God.

SCRIPTURE

Where you go, I will go; where you lodge, I will lodge; your people shall be my people, and your God my God.   *Ruth 1:16*

MEDITATION

My place is with the people of God. As I end my day in reflection and prayer, for others the day begins. Their pilgrimage is mine, too. God who is God in their hardships and their hopes, is God also in mine. No longer am I alone; nor is the tortured Christian, the starving believer. They are my people; with them I too belong to God.

PRAYER

Where they go, I will go. God of our journey, lead me to the place of compassion, where I may care more for the needs of others than about my own troubles. Teach me to share what I have, and to dwell among your people, the poor, the humble, the hungry and thirsty for justice; through Jesus Christ our Lord.

A LAST PRAYER

As I sleep, grant me rest. When I rise, grant me strength. In all my living, O God, be my God, and your people my people.

Day 5 ✸ *Morning*

The Lord is my light and my salvation; whom shall I fear? The Lord is the stronghold of my life; of whom shall I be afraid?

Psalm 27:1

SCRIPTURE

God called to Moses out of the bush, 'Moses, Moses!' And he said, 'Here I am.' Then he said, 'Come no closer! Remove the sandals from your feet, for the place on which you are standing is holy ground.' *Exodus 3:4b–5*

MEDITATION

Whenever God calls us by name, we must be ready to respond. But God is not to be trifled with. Where God stands is holy ground, and we must not trample all over the place in dirty boots. Today God may call me by name through someone in authority over me, or through someone in need of me, or through my newspaper or television. I must be ready, and stand barefoot at the sound of God's voice, alert to serve as I am asked.

Picture those whom you know will ask for your service today. Pray for them, and for those who will call on you without warning. Seek the blessing of God for them.

PRAYER FOR TODAY

I am here, at your call. I am waiting for your command. Make me a cheerful servant in all I do. And give me the grace to thank those who, in shop and bus, in hospital and filling station, wait on me today; through Jesus Christ our Lord.

THE LORD'S PRAYER

Day 5 ● Evening

To you, O Lord, I lift up my soul. O my God, in you I trust; do not let me be put to shame; do not let my enemies exult over me.   *Psalm 25:1–2*

Perhaps today, which started out with such great promise, fell flat. People were awkward and I lost sight of God in them. My irritation became angry words or dark thoughts. Yet now I must remember this: I am more ready to give up on myself than God is to abandon me.

SCRIPTURE
The saying is sure and worthy of full acceptance, that Christ Jesus came into the world to save sinners.   *1 Timothy 1:15*

MEDITATION
The purpose of God is to save the world. I know this because of what I see in the Gospels of Jesus. Here is real hope for me. I have tried to live God's way in my strength, and I have failed. If this were the end of the story, it would be a tragedy. Thank God for good news (gospel), and thank God that it is gospel not just for me but for all those I have met today.

PRAYER
It has not all been bad, dear God, not all. But some of today must have broken your heart, and for my part in that I ask your forgiveness. Forgive me for my casual greed, my insensitivity to the hurts of others; renew your broken world and cleanse the dirtiness of our living; through Jesus Christ our Lord.

A LAST PRAYER
As my day draws to its close, and my eyelids close in sleep, open to me your arms of mercy. While I lie still this night, guard me and your whole world from all harm and danger, all violence and oppression, all fear and distrust.

Day 6 ❋ Morning

O sing to the Lord a new song; sing to the Lord, all the earth.
Psalm 96:1

SCRIPTURE
Let love be genuine; hate what is evil, hold fast to what is good.
Romans 12:9

MEDITATION
Everyone agrees that love is a virtue. How can I love the unlovely? Only by being rooted in God. Love is part of the fruit of the Spirit. Fruits come from roots. Tying apples on a tree does not make an apple tree. I cannot tie love on to myself; I must be rooted (grafted) into God. If I am to resist temptation and do what is good, I need the strength of God today.

Imagine a plant in a dry land in search of water. Deeper and deeper its roots go in search of life. You are that plant; root yourself deeply in God, so that others may be refreshed by the fruit of love you bear for them.

PRAYER FOR TODAY
I am thirsty, and the world is thirsty too. We are thirsty for your love.

THE LORD'S PRAYER

Day 6 ☽ Evening

For God alone my soul waits in silence, for my hope is from
him.
Psalm 62:5

*I am still thirsty, dear God. I am drained and dry. I am weary
and faint. I poured myself out for you, and there is nothing left.
I have no words, only an emptiness. So I wait for the hope which
is nothing other than emptiness before God.*

SCRIPTURE
Those who drink of the water I will give them will never be
thirsty. The water that I will give will become in them a spring
of water gushing up to eternal life.
John 4:14

MEDITATION
Can life really bubble up in me? Yes. Jesus promises that not
only my thirst will be slaked, but that others too can be
refreshed—for I am not simply to be filled like a cup, I am to
become a source of the water of life for others.

PRAYER
So many things, so many people have demanded my attention
today. And now I cry to you, and demand your attention. Give
me grace to wait a while, so that I may be ready to receive you;
through Jesus Christ our Lord.

A LAST PRAYER
Now I am still, and in the silence you are here. Be close to those
for whom the busy-ness of day begins.

Day 7 ✳ Morning

Bless the Lord, O my soul. O Lord my God, you are very great. You are clothed with honour and majesty, wrapped in light as with a garment. You stretch out the heavens like a tent.

Psalm 104:1–2

SCRIPTURE

Those of steadfast mind you keep in peace—in peace because they trust in you. *Isaiah 26:3*

MEDITATION

So many things in life conspire to overturn me. Today I must be steadfast, anchored to God, so that when the storms come I am kept in peace. My temper, my irritation can be overcome, if I entrust myself to God's keeping power. At the flashpoints today, I will turn from the heat of the situation to the light of God in Christ.

Remember those who most often upset you. Take all that you would like to say to them, and offer them the peace of Christ instead. Pray that you may be consistent to all, and steadfast in God.

PRAYER FOR TODAY

How easily I flare up, dear Lord! How quickly I am roused! Keep me today in your steady peace, so that I may be of use to you and of service to all I meet; through Jesus Christ our Lord.

THE LORD'S PRAYER

Day 7 ☽ Evening

Restore us, O God; let your face shine, that we may be saved.

Psalm 80:3

Today was a day for being steady. What happened? Was it really all everyone else's fault? Was I like Peter, too ready to notice the waves to see Jesus? Yet still God's arm stretches out to save me. There is a hope beyond my despair.

SCRIPTURE

I have loved you with an everlasting love. *Jeremiah 31:3*

MEDITATION

God's love is unswerving, even when I am deflected from my highest resolve. I cannot allow this to leave me unchanged. My failure cannot simply be forgotten. I need the love of God to change and transform me. Yet this God can do—even for me.

PRAYER

Teach me, Saviour, not to take your love for granted. Turn me from self-pity to a love for those who hurt me most. Show me how to take up my cross for others, and to find in the fury of the storm the peace that anchors me to you; through Jesus Christ our Lord.

A LAST PRAYER

The time to rest has come; let me rest in you. Guard those who begin their day as I end mine, and keep us all in your steadfast peace.

Day 8 ✳ *Morning*

I say to the Lord, 'You are my Lord; I have no good apart from
you.'
                                                         Psalm 16:2

SCRIPTURE
Seek the welfare of the city where I have sent you into exile,
and pray to the Lord on its behalf, for in its welfare you will
find your welfare.
                                                    Jeremiah 29:7

MEDITATION
Does daily life seem hard and unremitting, or friendless and
cheerless—almost like the loneliness of exile? Or can you
imagine how exiles or asylum seekers feel far from their home?
In this morning's scripture we are told to treasure our present
situation. It is no use wishing that I were somewhere else; I am
here. I cannot avoid the realities of every-day living. Instead of
moping and moaning, I must pray and work for my desert to
become God's garden.

*Offer to God for a blessing the place where you live (the house,
the street). Pray that your fellow citizens may find true pros-
perity in peace and justice, that all may be granted the dignity
of their creation by God.*

PRAYER FOR TODAY
Deliver me from criticizing everything around me. Teach me
how to work for the good of all I meet today, all whose stories I
read in the paper or see on the news. Deliver me from seeing
welfare as a hand-out. Teach me to love all your creation as you
do, without distinction and without preference; through Jesus
Christ our Lord.

THE LORD'S PRAYER

Day 8 ☾ *Evening*

Help me, O Lord my God! Save me according to your steadfast
love. *Psalm 109:26*

*The day, with all its opportunities, is drawing to a close.
Remember before God those you met today. Some people were
helpful; others were not. Yet it was the welfare of all that God
called us to seek. Acknowledge where that was left undone, and
resolve to show, as well as to know, God's steadfast love. As you
seek forgiveness, release those whom you have bound today.*

SCRIPTURE
Return to me, and I will return to you, says the Lord of hosts.
Malachi 3:7

MEDITATION
However far I have drifted, God waits for me. Like the prodigal
son, I have only to turn to discover the love of God. My welfare
is linked with the welfare of the world. When I turn from my
selfishness, I discover that in the well-being of others I find
God welcoming me to a feast. I am not on my own, I am in
community. Until they are well, I am never truly healed.

PRAYER
I have turned my back on others; turn me back to you. I have
lost sight of you; heal my blindness. I have stumbled alone; lead
me safely into the company of your people. I have turned my
back on others; turn me back to you; through Jesus Christ our
Lord.

A LAST PRAYER
As darkness falls, Lord, be my light. As morning comes for
others, Lord, be their salvation. O light and salvation of the
world, drive away fear and darkness from all people, and
deliver us from evil.

Day 9 ✳ Morning

The heavens are telling the glory of God; and the firmament
proclaims his handiwork.   *Psalm 19:1*

SCRIPTURE
Trust in the Lord with all your heart and do not rely on your
own insight. In all your ways acknowledge him and he will
make straight your paths.   *Proverbs 3:5–6*

MEDITATION
Here is the secret of integrity. Honesty and reliability depend on
more than personal judgement. We need humility before God,
and a recognition that without God we quickly go astray. If my
life today is to ring true, then I must be open to God in every
situation. I do not need to know everything before I start out; I
simply need at each step to acknowledge a wisdom beyond my
own.

*As you begin this day, you may be aware of decisions you have
to make. Place the issues and the people before God now;
nothing is too big or too small. Perhaps you have no idea what
today will bring. Set your uncertainty in the hands of God. If
you have skills which put you in control, acknowledge your
limitations. If you feel inadequate, seek the wisdom which God
alone can give.*

PRAYER FOR TODAY
Here I am, Lord. There you are. Lead me from self-confidence
to reliance on you, so that today I may be of service and value
to those I meet; through Jesus Christ our Lord.

THE LORD'S PRAYER

Day 9 ☽ *Evening*

The Lord is merciful and gracious, slow to anger and abounding in steadfast love. *Psalm 103:8*

How quick I am to take offence, to nurse my hurt, and feed my grudges. Yet how speedily I want release from my guilt. It is not enough to see the distance between myself and God, I must not resist God who has come near to me in Jesus. I need conversion as well as forgiveness.

SCRIPTURE

I, I am he who blots out your transgressions for my own sake, and I will not remember your sins. *Isaiah 43:25*

MEDITATION

We are forgiven not because we deserve it, nor because God is weakened by our misery. We are forgiven, because God's nature is to put things right, not simply to write them off. At the end of this day here is the gospel not just for me, but for the world. Forgiveness does not come because God has forgotten; God forgets because first we are forgiven.

PRAYER

Teach me to take my sinfulness seriously, not to make light of what lies heavy in the lives of others. Teach me the joy of repentance, and the release of forgiveness, so that I may offer them to others. For am I bound not least by my own hard-heartedness; through Jesus Christ our Lord.

A LAST PRAYER

Remember me, loving God, as I sleep, and remember those for whom the coming hours are full of danger or distress. Stand close beside those who die this night, and bring us all into the liberty of your eternal presence.

Day 10 ✳ *Morning*

I lift up my eyes to the hills—from where will my help come?
My help comes from the Lord, who made heaven and earth.

Psalm 121:1–2

SCRIPTURE

Jesus found Philip and said to him, 'Follow me.'   *John 1:43*

MEDITATION

The word of Jesus is so simple: 'Follow me.' So often we want
Jesus to come with us, to be a lucky charm, so that we can play
with fire without getting hurt. Yet Jesus asks us to go with him.
If today I am truly to be a Christian, I must be a follower.

*Can I give up my independence and be a disciple? If I am self-
reliant, how can I depend on God? And if I do not depend on
God, do I not separate myself from the place of my help and
safety?*

PRAYER FOR TODAY

Lead me where you will, and give me grace to follow. Keep me
close enough to hear the quiet voice of conscience and to see
your footsteps in the dust of my daily life. When you reach out
to me in the hand of the beggar or the cry of the lonely, teach me
not to walk on when you have stopped; through Jesus Christ our
Lord.

THE LORD'S PRAYER

Day 10 ☽ *Evening*

O Lord, God of my salvation, when, at night, I cry out in your presence, let my prayer come before you; incline your ear to my cry. *Psalm 88:1–2*

Has prayer been hard today? Has the routine of life dulled me to insensitivity? Have the demands of others tired me out? Has the emptiness of my room become the emptiness of my life? I cry out to God that I may be renewed. What I can say to no one else, I whisper to the One who made me.

SCRIPTURE

Come to me, all you that are weary and are carrying heavy burdens, and I will give you rest. *Matthew 11:28*

MEDITATION

Strength enough for this burden, light enough for this step, courage enough for this moment—these are the promises of Jesus for me. In my weariness and exhaustion I find refreshment here and now. Yes, tomorrow has its cares; but now, with all those who are worn out, I turn to Christ for rest.

PRAYER

This heavy load is mine, but now I set it down. My restlessness I bring to you. What I dare not confess even to those who love me most, I acknowledge to you. Hear the cry of those whose burden is greater than mine, whose anxiety is deeper than mine, whose secrets are darker than mine. Bring us all to the rest that we have failed to find, and grant us peace; through Jesus Christ our Lord.

A LAST PRAYER

Fill my thoughts and dreams with the love, joy and peace of the Holy Spirit. To your world give hope, and to those who take up the burdens of a new day grant strength and courage.

Day 11 ✳ Morning

O give thanks to the Lord, for he is good; for his steadfast love
endures forever.   *Psalm 107:1*

SCRIPTURE
Be strong and courageous; do not be frightened for the Lord
your God is with you wherever you go.   *Joshua 1:9*

MEDITATION
These words were spoken to Joshua as he took on an over-
whelming task. Over and above his own personal courage, he
needed other resources. This scripture is not a rubber stamp of
divine approval for our own selfishness. At the beginning of
each day I need to be determined to do God's will. Then,
however great the difficulties, I can draw my strength and my
courage from God's presence with me.

*When you are tempted to think that, because you cannot do
much, you might as well do nothing, stop and think. Remember
that meeting this challenge will strengthen you for the next.
Seek the courage you do not have from God, who does.*

PRAYER FOR TODAY
You know the difficulties I face, and the excuses I make. I will
dare most things for those I love. Teach me to love those for
whom I dare little. Teach me to love you; through Jesus Christ
our Lord.

THE LORD'S PRAYER

Day 11 ☽ Evening

Happy are those whose transgression is forgiven, whose sin is covered.

Psalm 32:1

As you think back over the day, what hurts most? The failure which has pricked your own self-esteem, or the hurt you have caused others? Or is it those pressures of the way the world is which have squeezed you and distorted human values? This brokenness in ourselves, in those we meet, in our structures, in our world, needs repair. We need putting right. The good news is that God has acted decisively to do this.

SCRIPTURE

While we were still weak, at the right time Christ died for the ungodly.

Romans 5:6

MEDITATION

The ungodly are not just those who know about God but ignore what they know. It includes those who do not know at all. God's forgiveness is not for those who 'deserve' it. It is for all. How have I shared this forgiveness with the ungodly today? Can I really seek forgiveness for myself if I withhold it from others?

PRAYER

I have confused hard-headedness with hard-heartedness. I have told myself that my coldness was 'realism'. Renew me, so that I may bring your forgiveness to all I meet. Teach me not to count up my injuries, but to find healing in you.

A LAST PRAYER

Slowly the day closes, the rush subsides, the stillness comes. Fill the silence with your presence, and be with all who keep me safe while I sleep.

Day 12 ✳ *Morning*

Praise the Lord! How good it is to sing praises to our God; for he is gracious, and a song of praise is fitting.

Psalm 147:1

SCRIPTURE

Trust in the Lord for ever, for in the Lord God you have an ever-lasting rock.

Isaiah 26:4

MEDITATION

So often we think of God as distant, remote. This scripture tells us that God is the rock under our feet. We can walk with confidence, when we put our confidence in God. The strength of faith is not demonstrated by how firm our belief is but by how reliable is the ground of our trust. We have more confidence in the rock than the quicksand; and it is the rock which gives its strength to our faith. So too with God. I do not need to screw up my faith, my strength comes from the Rock.

Concentrate for a moment on the first decision you will make today. Stand firm on the rock and make a steady survey of the options. So long as you are on the rock, your footing is sure and you are free to scan the horizon without fear.

PRAYER FOR TODAY

You are the ground on which I stand firm. Keep me from wandering astray, and losing my way. Give me grace to share this ground with all I meet today; through Jesus Christ our Lord.

THE LORD'S PRAYER

Day 12 ☽ Evening

For your steadfast love is as high as the heavens; your faithfulness extends to the clouds.   *Psalm 57:10*

As far as I can see, and beyond, God's love holds steady. When today I have been fickle, God has been faithful; when I have stumbled, God has held firm. In my living today, have I obscured the consistent, purposeful love of God? I remember the day, and offer myself and all I have done or been for God's renewal.

SCRIPTURE
A new heart I will give you, and a new spirit I will put within you; and I will remove from your body the heart of stone and give you a heart of flesh.   *Ezekiel 36:26*

MEDITATION
God promises us not simply the opportunity to turn over a new leaf, but the means of living in a radically different way. So often my best efforts fail because 'my heart isn't in it'. Now God's heart can be in me. The love of God which filled the life of Jesus is given to me.

PRAYER
Living flame of holy love, burn in me. Shine through me and banish the darkness which threatens to smother my love for others; through Jesus Christ our Lord.

A LAST PRAYER
The end of my day is here, but others are beginning theirs. While I sleep and they wake, keep us all in your steadfast love. Give to the weak strength and to the strong grace, that your world may sing your praise eternally.

Day 13 ✳ *Morning*

'Be still, and know that I am God! I am exalted among the nations, I am exalted in the earth.'   *Psalm 46:10*

SCRIPTURE

Blessed are those who hear the word of God and obey it.

Luke 11:28

MEDITATION

How easy it is to read or hear the words of scripture and to forget them! Jesus tells an enthusiastic listener that real blessing comes from perseverance. The words of Jesus may move us with their beauty or their high ideals; but, if the emotional charge does not lead to action, the effect is like a blank cartridge—a flash of noise and smoke and no more.

To be still today will require concentration. Before we are swept up in the rush of events, we need to be still and know that God is God. In all the urgent claims on our time, our attention, and our loyalties, we must discern what is of central importance. For this we need stillness, the stillness of the centre around which events whirl, the stillness of God who moves with purpose and not at the tug of the loudest or latest voice.

PRAYER FOR TODAY

When you spoke, creating God, you brought order out of chaos. Bring order to my life, that I may not be distracted by the noise and confusion of the urgent only to lose sight of the important. In all the clamour help me hear your voice, and when I hear give me the grace to obey; through Jesus Christ our Lord.

THE LORD'S PRAYER

Day 13 ◐ *Evening*

But you, O Lord, are a God merciful and gracious, slow to anger and abounding in steadfast love and faithfulness.

Psalm 86:15

In these silent moments, recall the mercy of God to you this day. In the worst of it you were not abandoned, in the best of it you were not alone. Where you were hasty, God relented; where you were deflected, God held firm.

SCRIPTURE

Shall not the Judge of all the earth do what is just?

Genesis 18:25

MEDITATION

As I look at the world, as I read the papers and watch the news, so much seems to be unfair, unjust. If I am tempted to despair, or to lose faith in God, these words of Abraham come to strengthen me. There is a justice in the world which is more than revenge, and God is at work. The presence in our world of those who hunger and thirst to see right prevail is part of God's march to justice. The judge of all the earth will do right.

PRAYER

God of justice, deliver me from hot revenge. Free your world from angry violence. Bring to nothing the ends of those who plan evil and mischief, bring to plenty those who hunger and thirst in the cause of the right; through Jesus Christ our Lord.

A LAST PRAYER

My day is ended, and yet my work remains. Give me grace to leave what is done to your care, and strength to take up again what remains. Comfort those who are losing heart, and give to your world the justice that is salvation.

Day 14 ✳ Morning

O come, let us worship and bow down, let us kneel before the
Lord, our Maker!   *Psalm 95:6*

SCRIPTURE
God saw everything that he had made, and indeed, it was very
good.   *Genesis 1:31*

MEDITATION
Sometimes we are tempted to look at the world and think it
wicked. 'The world has gone to the devil,' we say. Yet it is the
world of God's making, and God saw its goodness. Even at its
darkest moments, God's purpose has been to save it from its
self-destruction. This world in which we live is not so easily
cast away; the evil, the brokenness, the pain of the world are not
its purpose or its underlying nature. The cross of Jesus is not
just wickedness; for out of the horror of death God works to
bring our good.

*Do not condemn the world in which you live, or abandon it to
its fate. Instead, allow the death of Christ to work through you
for the good of others.*

PRAYER FOR TODAY
This world is the world you love. This world is the world you
are bringing to salvation. Teach me to love as you do, to work
as you do, so that your kingdom may come on earth and your
will be done as in heaven; through Jesus Christ our Lord.

THE LORD'S PRAYER

Day 14 ☽ *Evening*

Out of my distress I called on the Lord; the Lord answered me and set me in a broad place. *Psalm 118:5*

There are so many things for which to be thankful. Even in sorrow, we may know the sorrow of God alongside us. In pain we may be strengthened by the sufferings of Christ. Whether today has been good or bad, call now on God, who saves you.

SCRIPTURE
We are afflicted in every way, but not crushed; perplexed, but not driven to despair; persecuted, but not forsaken; struck down, but not destroyed; always carrying in the body the death of Jesus, so that the life of Jesus may also be made visible in our bodies. *2 Corinthians 4:8–10*

MEDITATION
'We are knocked down, but not knocked out.' It is not simply that I know victory after death 'in the spirit'; I can know the life of Jesus in my every-day, here-and-now life. My faith is not just for later. 'Hope deferred makes the heart sick.' My faith is for today, for this moment, now.

PRAYER
Beyond my sight, you see me. Beyond my hearing, you hear me. Beyond my words, you speak to me. Be present with those who feel abandoned, lift those who have fallen, stand beside those who are afraid this night; through Jesus Christ our Lord.

A LAST PRAYER
As I turn out the light, be the light that the night cannot master. Be the radiance of those whose life is set in darkness. Light of the world, be the life of humankind.

Day 15 ✳ Morning

From the rising of the sun to its setting the name of the Lord is
to be praised.   *Psalm 113:3*

SCRIPTURE

When you search for me, you will find me; if you seek me with
all your heart. I will let you find me, says the Lord.
                                                Jeremiah 29:13–14a

MEDITATION

Where do we look for God? In creation, the intricacy and
complexity of the world around us. In the poor and the needy
who long for justice. In the company of other believers. In the
voice of conscience. In the witness of scripture. There are so
many places in which to look for God. Why do we give up so
quickly?

*Offer this day to God, who will meet you in so many different
ways. Pray that you may be alert enough to see beyond the
surface of people and things. You will find the underlying
reality of God where you come to grips with the heart of the
matter.*

PRAYER FOR TODAY

God of the deeps, I skim over the surface and miss you entirely.
Plunge me into depths; and, when I am out of my depth, speak
to me, heart to heart; through Jesus Christ our Lord.

THE LORD'S PRAYER

Day 15 ☽ Evening

To you, O Lord, I call; my rock, do not refuse to hear me, for if you are silent to me, I shall be like those who go down to the Pit.   *Psalm 28:1*

Take time now to listen. Focus your attention carefully. As your thoughts and imagination carry you through today's events, listen to the underlying voice, the deeper questions. Offer this listening to God, and be still. For God is listening too.

SCRIPTURE

Even to your old age I am he, even when you turn grey I will carry you. I have made, and I will bear; I will carry and will save.   *Isaiah 46:4*

MEDITATION

God will carry me. I have burdens of my own to carry, but God is not among them. God will carry me with all my load. So long as I cling on to my anxieties, my religion is idolatry; I will be carrying my image of God around with all the rest of my distress. My god will become additional weight. God calls me to come empty-handed, and to discover the gift of freedom.

PRAYER

I have not made you. You have made me. Deliver me from the burdens that have exhausted me. Carry those whom anxiety has brought to premature age. Support the weak and the weary. Set us all in the safety of your strong love; through Jesus Christ our Lord.

A LAST PRAYER

I rest in you, my God; grant me peace. Speak quietly to those who lie restless, and give your strength to those who at this hour take up again their responsibilities.

Day 16 ✳ Morning

Your word is a lamp to my feet and a light to my path.

Psalm 119:105

SCRIPTURE

I have called you by name; you are mine. When you pass
through the waters, I will be with you; and through the rivers,
they shall not overwhelm you; when you walk through the fire
you shall not be burned, and the flame shall not consume you.

Isaiah 43:1c–3a

MEDITATION

This is not an invitation to play with fire, and trust that there
will be no consequences! This morning's scripture is a fresh
invitation to trust God. When those things we cannot control
and cannot avoid threaten to overturn me, God will be there. I
do not need to run away; because God knows me and calls me
by name, all that today brings I can face with confidence.

*Call to mind the people and events you would rather avoid, but
cannot. Confront them not in fear but with love. These trials are
stepping stones with God and to God.*

PRAYER FOR TODAY

When others call me names, you call me by name. When
fire and flood come, you are there. For others, too, there are
fears and trials. Grant that I may not avoid the place where they
are and where you are; through Jesus Christ our Lord.

THE LORD'S PRAYER

Day 16 ☽ *Evening*

Guard me as the apple of the eye; hide me in the shadow of your
wings.   *Psalm 17:8*

*Perhaps you are feeling small and unimportant at the end of
this day. You have been overlooked, ignored, slighted. How
painful this is! Do not hide your hurt, but do not allow the
wounds to be poisoned by resentment. Turn to God, and hide
yourself in the love which protects and guards you.*

SCRIPTURE
Once you were not a people, but now you are God's people;
once you had not received mercy, but now you have received
mercy.   *1 Peter 2:10*

MEDITATION
These words of 1 Peter remind me that I am part of the body of
Christ. I am not alone however isolated I feel. Nor have I been
abandoned to my fate. God has brought me to a place of mercy,
the cross of Christ. The place where love defeats the very worst
evil can do. If this is true for me, it is true for the persecuted, the
tortured, the forsaken. Their place is with me, and mine is with
them—all one in Christ Jesus.

PRAYER
Shed your mercy on those who are sore with the harshness of
the world. As I look for mercy, make me merciful. Teach me the
generosity of love which makes me a spendthrift and enriches
your world; through Jesus Christ our Lord.

A LAST PRAYER
Keep your world safe this night, loving God, and bring us all to
the peace which makes us children of yours.

Day 17 ✳ Morning

O taste and see that the Lord is good.   *Psalm 34:8*

SCRIPTURE
Choose this day whom you will serve ... as for me and my
household, we will serve the Lord.   *Joshua 24:15*

MEDITATION
Joshua challenged his people to decide whom they would serve
if not the God who had brought them to freedom. For himself,
the issue is clear: other gods, local religions are not for him. We,
too, can be subject to the pressure to conform, to be like
everyone else.

*Choose again to follow the God who is revealed in Jesus, to be
Christ-like. By the grace of the Holy Spirit, resist revenge,
resentment, selfish ambition. Find God in humility, forgiveness
and friendship.*

PRAYER FOR TODAY
Where can I go but to you? As I start this day, how shall I
journey without the compass of your word? Keep me from
losing my temper, my sense of proportion, my values, my self.
Keep me from losing sight of you; through Jesus Christ our
Lord.

THE LORD'S PRAYER

Day 17 ☽ *Evening*

I will both lie down and sleep in peace; for you alone, O Lord, make me lie down in safety.   *Psalm 4:8*

You have come to this hour in safety, by the guiding hand of God. Where serving God has demanded resolution today, where it has been costly, give thanks that you have not always failed, and rest in the forgiveness of the one who keeps you safe tonight.

SCRIPTURE

My child, do not despise the Lord's discipline or be weary of his reproof, for the Lord reproves the one he loves, as a father the son in whom he delights.   *Proverbs 3:11–12*

MEDITATION

Some fathers are wicked, some fathers abuse their children, some are violent, some are oppressors. God's word of correction is not the anger that destroys, but the love that suffers and puts right. I need not be fearful, for God's perfect love for me and in me casts fear away.

PRAYER

You have corrected me, and I have found it hard. Yet you have not rejected me, and your arm reaches out to enfold me. Deliver from oppression those whose parents are always angry, always destructive. Restrain in me and in others the desire to punish, to crush. Teach your world the way of justice and of love. Correct in us the urge to harm and to maim, heal us and make us a place of healing; through Jesus Christ our Lord.

A LAST PRAYER

As I sleep, do not sleep yourself, dear God. Watch your world when no one else will look, and deliver us from evil.

Day 18 ❋ *Morning*

Blessed be the Lord, the God of Israel, who alone does wondrous things.   *Psalm 72:18*

SCRIPTURE
I will rejoice in the Lord; I will exult in the God of my salvation
Habakkuk 3:18

MEDITATION
Underneath the circumstance of life lies the foundation on which I am being built, and that foundation is Jesus Christ. Here is cause for a joy and delight beyond happiness in success or disappointment in failure. I need not go around with an empty grin on my face, but deep down I can rejoice in God who is my true security.

In the stillness name before God those people and those things that so often darken your days. Bring them into the light, and rejoice in that light of God which banishes the darkness.

PRAYER FOR TODAY
As you shine in me, shine through me. May I bring the gladness of your presence to others by my sympathy in their adversities and your courage in mine; through Jesus Christ our Lord.

THE LORD'S PRAYER

Day 18 ☽ Evening

Our help is in the name of the Lord, who made heaven and earth.

Psalm 124:8

God is bigger than our problems. This may seem obvious, but how often we forget. The God whom we worship sustains the universe and sets it free. The complexities of your life are not beyond God. Here you find help and hope.

SCRIPTURE

Come, let us return to the Lord; for it is he who has torn, and he will heal us; he has struck down, and he will bind us up.

Hosea 6:1

MEDITATION

My failures and their consequences are not God's last word. As I think over this day, I can come to God, the surgeon whose knife heals. Jesus talks of God as a gardener who has a pruning knife, which either cuts off or cuts back. What hurts now is for my ultimate fruitfulness. God is not vindictive, but is looking for vigorous life in me.

PRAYER

I am here, loving God. I am broken, mend me; I have fallen, set me on my feet; I am fearful, fill me with your love. I have broken others, forgive me and help me mend relationships. I have tripped up others, grant me grace to help them stand again. I have caused others to fear, teach me to love them; through Jesus Christ our Lord.

A LAST PRAYER

Quieten me, as a mother calms her child. Send your healing on this broken world, that the fallen may stand and the weary find rest.

Day 19 ✳ *Morning*

I will sing to the Lord, because he has dealt bountifully with me.   *Psalm 13:6*

SCRIPTURE
The kingdom of heaven is like a merchant in search of fine pearls; on finding one of great value, he went and sold all that he had and bought it.   *Matthew 13:45–46*

MEDITATION
Jesus' story of the jewel merchant tells of a trader who sells his entire stock in order to purchase one stone of surpassing excellence. The perfect enactment of God's will on earth is worth all that I can ever hoard or treasure. An old Jewish teacher said that if one person could keep the law of God perfectly for one day the Messiah would come. The presence of Jesus demands our very best and our greatest effort.

As you sit quietly now, gather your thoughts together and consider the task of doing God's will today. The responsibilities of justice and peace begin in our relationships with others. The kingdom of God comes by our determination to count everything else as unimportant in the pursuit of this goal. Love of God, love of neighbour, love of enemy—these are the will of God for me.

PRAYER FOR TODAY
There is so much that I value—my health, my sanity, my dreams. Give me grace above these to place the welfare of others, the willing service of those around me, the kingdom of God; through Jesus Christ our Lord.

THE LORD'S PRAYER

Day 19 ☽ Evening

The Lord is a stronghold for the oppressed, a stronghold in times of trouble.
Psalm 9:9

The poor and stranger have not been far away. Their dull eyes have stared at you in the street, in the paper, on television. They have looked for a stronghold, and you have had the opportunity to help give them some relief, some hope.

SCRIPTURE
Truly, I tell you just as you did it to one of the least of these ... you did it to me.
Matthew 25:40

MEDITATION
I have not always seen Jesus today—even when he looked at me and I at him. I have been embarrassed, dismissive, caught up in other things, in grander schemes. Yet by the mercy of God, I have not missed him every time, and tomorrow he awaits me and gives me the chance to love him aright.

PRAYER
I thought today ordinary, and I looked for you in out-of-the-ordinary places. You waited for me in the same old places, in the same old faces, in the same old ways. Teach me that it is in the ordinary things that you will make something out-of-the-ordinary; through Jesus Christ our Lord.

A LAST PRAYER
Deliver me from evil, free me from guilt, that I may rest and rise renewed to do your will. As others waken now, meet them in their daily routine and transform your world by those who keep your word.

Day 20 ✳ *Morning*

O give thanks to the Lord, for he is good; his steadfast love
endures forever!   *Psalm 118:1*

SCRIPTURE

Whoever wishes to be first among you must be slave of all. For
the Son of Man came not to be served but to serve, and to give
his life a ransom for many.   *Mark 10:44–45*

MEDITATION

How we like to be first, to be noticed. This longing lies deep
within us. When children pick teams, those who are left till last
feel deeply hurt. Yet Jesus warns us that greatness and grandeur
are not the same in God's scale of values. It is easy to say we
believe this, yet still to demand recognition, to avoid being
overlooked. Can Jesus' word change my living today?

*Make a list of those whom you know to be truly great. What
marks them out? Is it the way that they strut across the earth, or
is it the way they serve those who lie in the dust? Offer yourself
this day to God.*

PRAYER FOR TODAY

Show me how to change the world by service. Teach me how to
obey when I would rather give the orders. Make me a blessing
to those whom I so often ignore; through Jesus Christ our Lord.

THE LORD'S PRAYER

Day 20 ☽ *Evening*

Be pleased, O God, to deliver me. O Lord, make haste to help me!
Psalm 70:1

We cannot expect God to prevent our actions from having their consequences, for the creation is governed by cause and effect. We can ask God to deliver us from our waywardness and our disobedience. Often we need resources beyond ourselves to stand firm. For this grace we can cry out to God.

SCRIPTURE

I will heal their disloyalty; I will love them freely, for my anger has turned from them … They shall again live beneath my shadow, they shall flourish as a garden.
Hosea 14:5, 7

MEDITATION

It is at the root of the problem that I need the changing power of God. I am like an overrun garden, where the weeds have grown deep and smothered the beauty that was planned. God's word comes to me tonight to give me hope that all is not lost.

PRAYER

I have let myself go, and I have not shown to others the wonder of your love and the brightness of your face. They have lived in darkness because I have grown dark and have obscured your glory. Have mercy on me, for the health and welfare of others; through Jesus Christ our Lord.

A LAST PRAYER

I am weary, refresh me. I am weak, revive me. Renew the face of the earth, O God, and make me a part of your new creation. To all who toil this night give strength to do your will on earth as in heaven.

Day 21 ✳ Morning

Let the peoples praise you, O God; let all the peoples praise
you.   *Psalm 67:3*

SCRIPTURE
'I am the light of the world. Whoever follows me will never
walk in darkness but will have the light of life.'   *John 8:12*

MEDITATION
How do I see my religion? Is my faith just for me or for the
world? Jesus describes himself as the light of the world. He is
the light which dispels the darkness in which evil flourishes; he
is the light which brings creation to life, and to which life itself
stretches out with yearning. And I am to know and to show that
light.

*Before the rush of the day, acknowledge the pull of the darkness
in your own life and in the world. As you do, call on God to be
the light of the world for you and all you meet today.*

PRAYER FOR TODAY
God of the light, shine in me and through me, so that what is
evil is driven away. Draw me to yourself, and draw others with
me, so that we may grow in the light which gives the true life to
all created things; through Jesus Christ our Lord.

THE LORD'S PRAYER

Day 21 ◐ *Evening*

Restore us, O God of hosts; let your face shine, that we may be saved. *Psalm 80:7*

The light of God, which has been the theme of this day, reveals what has gone wrong, and reminds us of our need to be made anew. But the light of God is the beam of mercy, the smile of salvation, which welcomes us home. Do not run away, look on the face of God and live.

SCRIPTURE

If you forgive the sins of any, they are forgiven them; if you retain the sins of any, they are retained. *John 20:23*

MEDITATION

What we crave for ourselves is what others crave from us. These words of Jesus are addressed to his people in every age. When we lock people up in our unwillingness to forgive, they are imprisoned in fear, in hatred, in anger, in revenge. The calling of Christians is forgiveness. This is not cheap, it is painful. It costs us our self-righteousness, it costs us our hurts and scars. It cost Jesus his life.

PRAYER

I find it hard to forgive. Why should they get away with it? Why should they not suffer—just a little? Yet my pain is your pain, and the hurt I nurse is not healed until I cease from probing it. Break the bars of the prison I have made, that they and I may be free; through Jesus Christ our Lord.

A LAST PRAYER

I sleep, but you do not. You watch when I am unaware. Keep all your creation in the safety of your peace. Be close to those who tonight will bring to birth, to those who will be born.

Day 22 ✳ Morning

O Lord, our Sovereign, how majestic is your name in all the earth! You have set your glory above the heavens.   *Psalm 8:1*

SCRIPTURE
The steadfast love of the Lord never ceases, his mercies never come to an end; they are new every morning; great is your faithfulness.   *Lamentations 3:22–23*

MEDITATION
Every morning it is the same—God's love awaits me. In the routine of getting the day started I have an opportunity to respond to this love, which is always fresh and vibrant. Why am I in such a hurry that I can just brush past this extraordinary love of God? Does my failure to acknowledge the One who knows me best and loves me most mean that I also fail to love those who need my care and attention?

Stop the onward rush of your mind, allow the love of God to take possession of you. Now allow the faces of those you will meet today to become pictures of the face of God, who loves you and seeks your love.

PRAYER FOR TODAY
How many new things get worn out, dear God! My new enthusiasms, my new possessions, my new resolutions. How different is your new love. Root me and ground me not in my own resources, but in the depth of your being; through Jesus Christ our Lord.

THE LORD'S PRAYER

Day 22 ◑ Evening

Trust in him at all times, O people; pour out your heart before
him; God is a refuge for us. *Psalm 62:8*

*Has the trust you have placed in others and they have placed in
you today been betrayed? When we feel let down, we can turn
to God who is our refuge. Acknowledge your hurt and disappointment, and find the shelter you need.*

SCRIPTURE

I have swept away your transgressions like a cloud, and your
sins like mist; return to me, for I have redeemed you.
Isaiah 44:22

MEDITATION

'Transgressions' are those occasions when we have gone too
far. Today I have gone too far, and not far enough. God knows,
and I cannot hide it. Now I can own up to what I have allowed
myself to do and become. In the telling there is not just
emotional release, but the cleansing power of God to change
me at the level of my action and will.

PRAYER

This day has held both good and bad; and you, O God, know it
all. Forgive what has gone wrong, and bless what has been
worthwhile. Clear my sight, and make my path plain to me.
Grant me the grace of true repentance and the joy of your
forgiveness; through Jesus Christ our Lord.

A LAST PRAYER

Many have helped me today; give them your blessing. Many
have brought me to this hour in safety; grant them your peace.
On those who have received far less than I have done, send your
salvation. Bring the kingdoms of this world into the kingdom of
Jesus your Son.

Day 23 ✳ Morning

For who in the skies can be compared to the Lord? Who among the heavenly beings is like the Lord?   *Psalm 89:6*

SCRIPTURE
You are a letter of Christ ... written not with ink but with the Spirit of the living God.   *2 Corinthians 3:3*

MEDITATION
How good it is to receive a letter from someone we love. Such a letter is cherished and read with care. The words on the page bring light to our eyes, and our faces shine with joy. I am God's letter to the world! Do people 'read' me with love and affection, or with anxiety and dread?

Think of those you know who long for good news, for encouragement, for hope. Name them before God, and offer yourself as God's letter to them this day.

PRAYER FOR TODAY
God of love, you speak in the silence of lonely hearts. Thank you for those who keep in touch with me, and who encourage me. Thank you for those who bring me these letters. May the gladness I know with the good news of others be the experience of those I meet today. Make me good news to them; through Jesus Christ our Lord.

THE LORD'S PRAYER

Day 23 ☽ *Evening*

I waited patiently for the Lord; he inclined to me and heard my cry.   *Psalm 40:1*

We complain that God does not listen. Perhaps we do not wait. Stop now; really stop. Sit quietly and listen to the sounds around you and within you. After you have poured out your misery, stay long enough to hear the voice of God.

SCRIPTURE

Heal me, O Lord, and I shall be healed; save me, and I shall be saved; for you are my praise.   *Jeremiah 17:14*

MEDITATION

If I will accept the healing of God which goes to the heart of things, I shall be truly healed. Then I shall understand how God is my praise.

PRAYER

Beneath the surface, beyond the limits which we set, you are there. In the pain and disease of the world, at the root of the matter, you are there. I have been in such a hurry, that I have missed you. Slow me down, O God. Bring your world from its frenzied activity to the still centre where you dwell and where you work the healing and salvation of the nations.

A LAST PRAYER

Darkness comes, tiredness comes, rest comes. Yet for others, the darkness brings no rest, no relief. For those who work this night, I offer thanks. They bring my food to the stores, they clean the streets I walk, they bring the news I read and watch, they sit beside the ill and dying, they debate through the small hours the details of peace, they defend us against the assaults of the violent. Keep them safe in the peace which is beyond our gift and imagining.

Day 24 ✳ Morning

Great is the Lord, and greatly to be praised; his greatness is unsearchable.   *Psalm 145:3*

SCRIPTURE

Who is like the wise man? And who knows the interpretation of a thing? Wisdom makes one's face shine, and the hardness of one's countenance is changed.   *Ecclesiastes 8:1*

MEDITATION

What is this wisdom that transforms women and men? It is not ordinary (or extraordinary!) cleverness. No, this wisdom has its beginning in reverence for God. When we have brought our priorities into line with God's, we begin to walk the road to wisdom. An old tradition teaches that Jesus is supremely the Wisdom of God. Perhaps here is the key to this morning's scripture; when we are truly Christians (Christ's women and men) then we are transformed.

When I look at people, do I smile or do I frown? Do I welcome them or turn them away? If my face excludes people, how wise am I? Offer yourself to the wisdom of God this day. Make yourself an open door through which people may walk into the love of God.

PRAYER FOR TODAY

Teach me to be wise rather than clever, to be kind-hearted rather than hard-headed, to be transformed into the image of your Son. For he knew, but he understood as well; through Jesus Christ our Lord.

THE LORD'S PRAYER

Day 24 ◑ Evening

O give thanks to the Lord of lords, for his steadfast love endures
forever.   *Psalm 136:3*

*Our papers and our televisions are full of news about the
powerful and rich. How often they make themselves felt by their
possessions and their influence. God too is a ruler, a powerful
one; but the power of God is love, and the wealth of God is
generosity. At the end of this day give yourself into the hands of
this power and this wealth.*

SCRIPTURE
'Daughter, your faith has made you well; go in peace, and be
healed of your disease.'   *Mark 5:34*

MEDITATIONS
The words of Jesus were originally spoken to a woman whose
illness left her bodily weak, bankrupt and uncured, and reli-
giously disabled. Jesus saw in her desperation faith, and in that
faith the way back to a full life in the community. In God's
hands my desperation can become faith and the road back to a
healthy and fruitful life.

PRAYER
I turn to you, God of healing and wholeness. My life has
become fragmented and disordered, and my disarray has
brought confusion to others. Out of my chaos bring order, into
the life of the world send your peace; through Jesus Christ our
Lord.

A LAST PRAYER
I close my eyes, but watch over me. I rest, send me strength.
Your world awakes, renew it. It struggles for its liberation, send
it freedom.

Day 25 ✳ Morning

For your steadfast love is higher than the heavens, and your
faithfulness reaches to the clouds.   *Psalm 108:4*

SCRIPTURE
The disciples came to Jesus and asked, 'Who is the greatest in
the kingdom of heaven?' He called a child, whom he put among
them, and said, 'Truly I tell you, unless you change and become
like children you will never enter the kingdom of heaven.'
                                                    Matthew 18:1–3

MEDITATION
This is not an invitation to be childish, but to be childlike. One
of childhood's earliest sentences is, 'It's not fair!' Children
discern the difference between what we say and what we do,
and they condemn our hypocrisy. Jesus says that if we lose this
childlike singleness of vision we will miss the kingdom of God.
Today I need to see clearly, and to cease from the justifications
I offer for my fine words and weak actions.

*Think back to your childhood. Who were the adults you most
admired? Why? Are you like them?*

PRAYER FOR TODAY
Childlike God, I have so many excuses for the complications of
life. They do not convince me, and they do not convince you.
Teach me to live with singleness of vision, that I may see the
kingdom of heaven and show it to others; through Jesus Christ
our Lord.

THE LORD'S PRAYER

Day 25 ☽ Evening

Why are you cast down, O my soul, and why are you disquieted
within me? Hope in God; for I shall again praise him, my help
and my God. *Psalm 42:11*

*Disobedience, not doubt, is the enemy of faith. Doubt is like the
shadow which shows the sun is there. Artists can show sunlight
in two ways. Either they paint the direct glare of the sun, or they
make bold, deep shadows. Doubts are faith's shadows.*

SCRIPTURE

Jacob was left alone; and a man wrestled with him until
daybreak. When the man saw that he did not prevail against
Jacob, he struck him on the hip socket; and Jacob's hip was put
out of joint as he wrestled with him. Then he said, 'Let me go,
for the day is breaking.' But Jacob said, 'I will not let you go,
unless you bless me.' *Genesis 32:24–26*

MEDITATION

Jacob was trying to prevent his past from catching up with him.
He wrestled with his conscience, with the nightmare vision of
his brother seeking revenge, with God. The experience scarred
him for life, and ever after he limped. Was this a blessing in
disguise? When he met his brother, he was forgiven. I cannot
escape my past; but God can change my future, painful though
it may be. The limp may be the blessing, the wound may be the
cure.

PRAYER

I cling to you, God of my wrestling, for a blessing. Bless me,
and make me a blessing; through Jesus Christ our Lord.

A LAST PRAYER

To all those who fear, give courage. To all those who faint, grant
rest.

Day 26 ✳ *Morning*

But you, O Lord, are a shield around me, my glory, and the one who lifts up my head.

Psalm 3:3

SCRIPTURE

Where your treasure is, there your heart will be also.

Matthew 6:21

MEDITATION

What do I do with the money I have? How do I spend it? How do I save it? My answers will tell me what I consider important, my real driving passions. I can so easily convince myself that I am walking in God's way. Jesus offers this simple check. He invites us to look at the things we treasure. A bishop in the early Church was commanded by Roman troops to bring out the Church's treasure. He did so. Before the astonished soldiers he paraded the old and poor people of his congregation.

Stop for a moment to consider this challenge of Jesus. Think of the things you are saving for. Here is your treasure. Take today the opportunity to invest in God's way and purpose for the world. Give to the first person in need who confronts you today—not just your money, but your time, your skills, and your energies.

PRAYER

God of the poor, the treasure you offer is not power or influence. You give us one another to love. Give me time today to share the riches of your love with those who pull at my sleeve, who tug at my conscience. Teach me to give more than the spare change of my life to those in need; through Jesus Christ our Lord.

THE LORD'S PRAYER

Day 26 ☽ Evening

From the end of the earth I call to you, when my heart is faint.
Lead me to the rock that is higher than I; for you are my refuge,
a strong tower against the enemy. *Psalm 61:2–3*

*What happened to the resolutions made at the beginning of this
day? Do not give up on yourself, for God does not give up on
you. It is dangerous to wallow in guilt. Of course, some things
will have to change, but God will make those changes better in
the quiet than you will in the rush.*

SCRIPTURE
There will be more joy in heaven over one sinner who repents
than over ninety-nine righteous persons who need no repentance. *Luke 15:7*

MEDITATION
When something we have lost is found, how delighted we are.
We are more pleased about what we have found than we are
about the things we had not lost in the first place! Jesus says
that the same is true of God. How glad we ought to be when
someone apologizes to us, how free we ought to be with our
forgiveness and our delight! In this way we become more like
God, and God can do more with us.

PRAYER
I have been lost; you have found me. I have gone wrong; you
have turned me round. Turn me now to those I have wronged.
Teach me the joy of repentance and the delight of relationships
repaired; through Jesus Christ our Lord.

A LAST PRAYER
My day ends; others take up their duties. Give to us all the
vision of a world founded on justice, and of peoples dwelling in
peace.

Day 27 ✳ Morning

Make a joyful noise to the Lord, all the earth. Worship the Lord with gladness; come into his presence with singing.

Psalm 100:1–2

SCRIPTURE

Do not rob the poor because they are poor, or crush the afflicted at the gate; for the Lord pleads their cause and despoils the life of those who despoil them.

Proverbs 22:22–23

MEDITATION

Who is it who begs for money as you hurry past? Is it really the Lord God? When that dishevelled woman with her small child calls out, is that the voice of God? Was that card saying 'Homeless' a call from heaven?

In these moments of preparation for the day, remember the 'undeserving' poor. Why has God entrusted you with what you have? So that you may keep it for yourself and your best friends? Or so that you may copy the generosity of God, who sends blessings on just and unjust alike?

PRAYER FOR TODAY

Hungry God, you hunger for mercy. Make me generous this day as you call to me from the shop doorway. Shabby God, you shiver and ache. Grant me, who have eaten and clothed myself, the grace to give you warmth and shelter; through Jesus Christ our Lord.

THE LORD'S PRAYER

Day 27 ☽ Evening

As for me, I said, 'O Lord, be gracious to me; heal me, for I
have sinned against you.'   *Psalm 41:4*

*Our failures with one another are not private events, they touch
the being of God. Our anger, our greed, our self-righteousness
hurt God. As you think over the day, acknowledge the feelings
you have kept hidden but which have closed you off from
generosity, as well as the words and deeds that others have seen
and felt.*

SCRIPTURE
Forgetting what lies behind and straining forward to what lies
ahead, I press on towards the goal for the prize of the heavenly
call of God in Christ Jesus.   *Philippians 3:13–14*

MEDITATION
Here is good advice. How often I am held back by looking
back. Good athletes look for the finish and compete to the
end. Of course, I need to reflect on the past, but I need not
dwell on it. I can learn from what has happened without being
imprisoned by it.

PRAYER
Fix my attention, God of my goal, on you to whom I run so that
I may finish and not fall. Give me the strength and determination to keep my gaze on you, and make me of some use in your
world; through Jesus Christ our Lord.

A LAST PRAYER
As this day draws to its close and slips away, draw close to me
and do not let me slip far from you. For others the day is at its
height, keep them from falling. To all your world give peace in
these hours.

Day 28 ✳ Morning

The Lord is king, he is robed in majesty; the Lord is robed, he is girded with strength. He has established the world; it shall never be moved.   *Psalm 93:1*

SCRIPTURE
Look, I have set before you an open door, which no one is able to shut.   *Revelation 3:8*

MEDITATION
These words were spoken to Christians who felt weak, but who kept going. I may not be powerful, but I can be faithful, and God is making it easier for me by opening the door. What is more, no one else can close it. The opportunities I have today cannot be taken from me.

The chances God gives you are in the every-day situations of life. They are given you for serving God in friend and stranger. By a word or a kindly action you can transform someone's world today. As you do so, you will be joining God who is making all things new.

PRAYER FOR TODAY
God of the open door, give me the determination and grace to walk through to the new opportunity you offer me today. Give me the joy of sharing in the life of your kingdom, where those without hope may dream again, where those with no future find your great tomorrow; through Jesus Christ our Lord.

THE LORD'S PRAYER

Day 28 ☽ Evening

Return, O my soul, to your rest, for the Lord has dealt bountifully with you.

Psalm 116:7

*God is good. As the events of the day whirr through your head,
and you try to make sense of all that has happened, you can
rest. For God is good, and there is a generosity in the One who
has made us. Be still a moment, and allow God's rest to flood
into your heart and mind.*

SCRIPTURE

I am confident of this, that the one who began a good work
among you will bring it to completion by the day of Christ.

Philippians 1:6

MEDITATION

Even before I was aware of it, God was at work in me; and what
God has begun will not remain unfinished. I am being fashioned to become Christ-like, to display the love and goodness
of God in every part of my being. When the kingdom of God is
at last known and seen in all its fullness, I shall be caught up
with all creation in the worship and vision of God. This is the
goal.

PRAYER

Like a great artist you work at your creation, O God, losing
nothing and transforming everything. Shape us and set us to
display your glory here and now, so that what we now perceive
in part we may at last understand in full; through Jesus Christ
our Lord.

A LAST PRAYER

I rest in you, and find the peace that no one else can provide.
Give this same peace to all your world, and defend us from all
harm and evil, all sin and danger.

Day 29 ❋ Morning

Your throne, O God, endures for ever and ever.   *Psalm 45:6*

SCRIPTURE
My grace is sufficient for you, for my power is made perfect in
weakness.   *2 Corinthians 12:9*

MEDITATION
Each day there comes a moment when my weaknesses become
apparent to me. Yet in these moments all is not lost; for when
I cannot, God can. What is beyond me is not beyond God.
This morning's scripture invites me to call upon the resources
of God and to find strength and energy in weariness and
exhaustion.

Recall those occasions in the past when you have proved the
truth of these words. Now commit yourself into God's keeping,
God who has spoken to you. Once more you can rediscover this
unfailing source of vitality which will enable you to be God's
witness in the events of today.

PRAYER FOR TODAY
Vibrant God, source of life and goodness, flood through me
today, so that where I am weak your power to love and to
endure are displayed to those in need; through Jesus Christ our
Lord.

THE LORD'S PRAYER

Day 29 ☽ *Evening*

As far as the east is from the west, so far he removes our transgressions from us.

Psalm 103:12

God's way with your failings is to put them beyond your reach. When you have made your confession, you do not need to keep returning to the scene of the crime! Of course, you may need to put things right, but you do not need to keep accusing yourself.

SCRIPTURE

I will put my spirit within you and you shall live.

Ezekiel 37:14

MEDITATION

These words come from a vision of God breathing new life into bleached-out bones in the desert. Can God take my deadness and make me live? Yes, even this is not beyond God. More than this, the prophet saw that God can breathe life into a lifeless community. The world of which I am a part is not dead, without hope.

PRAYER

Into the dust you breathed life; into the bones you breathed your Spirit. Breathe into me, so that I may live to the full. Breathe into your world, that your whole creation may glorify you; through Jesus Christ our Lord.

A LAST PRAYER

As darkness falls, shine as the stars of the night. Drive from our homes the fears that come to haunt us. Give quietness of spirit to all who rest, and integrity of purpose to all who work.

Day 30 ✳ Morning

O Lord, how manifold are your works! In wisdom you have
made them all; the earth is full of your creatures.

Psalm 104:24

SCRIPTURE
Let your light shine before others, so that they may see your
good works and give glory to your Father in heaven.

Matthew 5:16

MEDITATION
The good things I do are not for my good first and foremost.
They are done for others, who give thanks not to me but to God.
I do like to be thanked, to be appreciated, but I can become big-
headed when I am praised, and grumpy when I am not! It is
much better for me that God should be glorified than that I
should be. It is better for those who give thanks, for they are
going to the root and source of all goodness when they praise
God.

*Offer yourself to do good and to be good for others without
looking for reward or advantage.*

PRAYER FOR TODAY
God of us all, you have shown us in Jesus how to bring hope
and goodness into the lives of others while giving the glory to
you. I am learning to walk in the way of Jesus. Keep me true to
him and to you; keep me open and alive to the longings and
needs of those I meet; and make me content to be a disciple, a
follower; through Jesus Christ our Lord.

THE LORD'S PRAYER

Day 30 ☽ *Evening*

O send out your light and your truth; let them lead me; let them
bring me to your holy hill and to your dwelling.   *Psalm 43:3*

*The light of God not only exposes darkness and deceit, it leads
to holiness. In all that has happened today, that light still shines
to lead you home to God. Make no excuses; do not resist; but as
you are led, follow.*

SCRIPTURE
Return to the Lord, your God, for he is gracious and merciful,
slow to anger, and abounding in steadfast love, and relents from
punishing.   *Job 2:13*

MEDITATION
God is not an ogre. How often I make God in my image, and
how often this god which I have made terrifies me! Yet God, in
whose image I am made, is painstaking with us, and is not
deflected from bringing all creation to its goal. The anger I fear
and the punishment I dread are far away. Make your prayer of
thanksgiving.

PRAYER
Again you have held me, and I have been kept even in the worst
that has happened. Receive my thanks, and grant me to share
with others the generosity I have received from you; through
Jesus Christ our Lord.

A LAST PRAYER
Goodnight, Lord God. I sleep, but you watch. Watch over your
world. Watch over those who are in danger. Watch over those
who keep us safe. I sleep, but you watch. Watch over me.

Day 31 ✳ Morning

Sing aloud to God our strength; shout for joy to the God of
Jacob. *Psalm 81:1*

SCRIPTURE
Jesus said, 'To what should I compare the kingdom of God? It
is like yeast that a woman took and mixed in with three
measures of flour until all of it was leavened.' *Luke 13:20*

MEDITATION
It takes very little yeast to raise a loaf. When I am tempted to
despair of the world, these words of Jesus encourage me. Those
small signs of justice and peace are the yeast of the kingdom of
God. This world will be changed by apparently small events.
The little I can do is still enough to change the world around
me. God is at work!

*Another day begins, and new opportunities for being God's
person in the world are yours. A smile instead of a frown, a kind
word instead of silence, silence instead of anger—these are the
tools you are given to shape God's world. Offer them with yourself as another day begins.*

PRAYER FOR TODAY
How different I wish the world was! How I would rearrange
things if I could! But this is the world you are at work in, Lord,
so change me and make me yeast in the bread; through Jesus
Christ our Lord.

THE LORD'S PRAYER

Day 31 ◐ Evening

Let the words of my mouth and the meditation of my heart be acceptable to you, O Lord, my rock and my redeemer.

Psalm 19:14

Take time to focus upon God. Do not rush. When we hurry we hardly ever hear what is said, and we nearly always fail to think things through. Meditating is not a high-speed activity. Think over the events of the day, and bring your thinking to God.

SCRIPTURE

Indeed, you are my lamp, O Lord, the Lord lightens my darkness. *2 Samuel 22:29*

MEDITATION

The lamp which is referred to here does not enable me to see for miles ahead. God's light shines in my immediate darkness. I see enough for the next few steps. I am not asked for blind faith nor am I granted complete foresight. Here and now God gives the light of conscience, of circumstances, of scripture, of the Spirit. It is all I need.

PRAYER

God of the light, shine in my darkness. God of the truth, speak in the silence. God of justice, teach me what is right. God of love, kindle your holy flame in all my ways and all my days; through Jesus Christ our Lord.

A LAST PRAYER

Give to me now the rest I need. Give to me the peace I seek. Grant to the powerful integrity, and bring the oppressed to the liberty and dignity of the children of God.

Special Feasts
and Seasons

Sunday ✳ *Morning*

Praise the Lord! Sing to the Lord a new song, his praise in the assembly of the faithful.   *Psalm 149:1*

SCRIPTURE

But you have come to Mount Zion and to the city of the living God, the heavenly Jerusalem, and to innumerable angels in festal gathering, and to the assembly of the firstborn who are enrolled in heaven, and to God the judge of all, and to the spirits of the righteous made perfect, and to Jesus, the mediator of a new covenant.   *Hebrews 12:22–24a*

MEDITATION

These words are a description of Sunday worship! On the first day of the week I am invited to join in the ceaseless activity of heaven. As I begin this day I am caught up into the vision of glory, and with me are the saints of every time and place. Together we sing; and all creation claps its hands and thunders out the praise of God.

Lift your face to the risen Christ; gaze on him, and open yourself to the glory he displays. Let the praises of God fill your mind and heart; and as they do, sing out the joy of the Lord.

PRAYER FOR TODAY

On this the first day you spoke, and the worlds began their being. On this the first day you spoke, and Jesus rose from the dead. On this the first day you spoke, and the Spirit filled the church. Speak this day, God of all that is, and bring your creation to life in you; through Jesus Christ our Lord.

THE LORD'S PRAYER

Sunday ☽ Evening

How lovely is your dwelling place, O Lord of hosts!

Psalm 84:1

The psalmist is describing the delight of a worshipper who climbs the hill of God and nears the summit. At last the goal is in sight, and the strenuous journey to God is about to be rewarded. Take time now to offer your own quiet praise for the glimpse you have had today of the glory that no words can properly describe, but which fills the heart, and lights the face, and brings us to perfect contentment.

SCRIPTURE

Day and night without ceasing they sing, 'Holy, holy, holy, the Lord God the Almighty, who was and is and is to come.'

Revelation 4:8b

MEDITATION

This is the song of those who stand in God's eternal presence. God, who began all things, is still at the centre of the creation, bringing it into being. God has not given up on what was begun; but more than this, God is the end in whom all things will find their purpose and fulfilment. Such is the God whom I, with all the company of heaven, have been worshipping today.

PRAYER

Holy God, your glory shines in the face of Jesus. Shine now in the darkness of the evening, and lighten all our ways with your praise; through Jesus Christ our Lord.

A LAST PRAYER

As I rest, others take up your praise. May all who sing your glory know you as their past, their present, their future; and as they enter that house which is your praise, may they give shelter and hope to those who have no home, no future, but you.

Advent ✳ *Morning*

Lift up your heads, O gates! and be lifted up O ancient doors!
that the King of glory may come in.   *Psalm 24:9*

SCRIPTURE
Sleeper, awake! Rise from the dead, and Christ will shine on
you.   *Ephesians 5:14b*

MEDITATION
Advent marks the Christian preparation for Christmas, when
we prepare ourselves for the coming of Jesus. We need to be
alert and on the watch for Christ wherever he meets us. In all
the rush to the festivities, we too can celebrate; but there is
more for me than this. There is the challenge to listen again to
scripture, to look again for the signs of God's kingdom in the
world.

*In this season of Advent, prepare for the light which shines in
your darkness. Be ready to turn from things you would rather
keep hidden, and to follow where Christ lights the way.*

PRAYER FOR TODAY
You ask me to wake up, Lord, to be awake to the world around
me and your presence in it. Show me your hidden self, the yeast
in the bread, where you work quietly and unnoticed in my life
and the lives of all people, in the life of the whole creation;
through Jesus Christ our Lord.

THE LORD'S PRAYER

Faithfulness will spring up from the ground, and righteousness will look down from the sky.   *Psalm 85:11*

God has sown faithfulness and righteousness in the person of Jesus. They challenge my life and the life of our world. God calls us to change our living to become like that of Jesus.

SCRIPTURE

The kingdom of God is as if someone would scatter seed on the ground, and would sleep and rise night and day, and the seed would sprout and grow, he does not know how .... But when the grain is ripe, at once he goes in with his sickle, because the harvest has come.   *Mark 4:26–27, 29*

MEDITATION

God has sown the seed of Jesus in the world, and the harvest is guaranteed. Advent reminds me that God is at work in me and in the world around me. There is a goal which God is shaping. I am called to share in planting faithfulness and righteousness in all my days and all my ways, so that the harvest may be plentiful.

PRAYER

For the coming of Jesus we thank you, God of salvation and harvest. For the call of Christ we praise you, God of the beginning and the end. Bring your world through the fire of judgement to the safety of your kingdom; through Jesus Christ our Lord.

A LAST PRAYER

I place my hope in you alone. In the darkness, keep alive the fire of your truth and the seed of your faithfulness, and give to your people this night the harvest of your Spirit—love, joy and peace.

Christmas Day ✳ *Morning*

O sing to the Lord a new song; make a joyful noise to the Lord, all the earth.

Psalm 98:1, 4a

SCRIPTURE
In the beginning was the Word, and the Word was with God, and the Word was God .... And the Word became flesh and dwelt among us. *John 1:1, 14*

MEDITATION
This is the first great feast day in the Church's year. With sisters and brothers across the world, I can remember that God is revealed uniquely in Jesus. Jesus was not born in a palace, but in a cattle-shed. God is with us all; kings and queens may come to a cattle-shed, but shepherds may not so easily go to palaces. We can never say to God, 'You do not understand', for God has dwelt among us! Peace on earth, and glory to God in the heavens!

PRAYER
You have made this day a feast for the hungry and a shelter for the homeless. As I celebrate, deliver me from feasting alone. As I share with friends, deliver me from excluding strangers. Fill me with praise like the angels, with curiosity like the shepherds, with trust like Joseph, and with grace like Mary; through Jesus Christ, babe of Bethlehem, hope of us all.

THE LORD'S PRAYER

Christmas Day ☽ *Evening*

I will give thanks to the Lord with my whole heart; I will tell of all your wonderful deeds. I will be glad and exult in you; I will sing praise to your name, O Most High.   *Psalm 9:1–2*

It has been a day of gifts and of feasting. In the Western tradition Christmas lasts for twelve days—until the Sixth of January. Eastern Christians keep that day as both Christmas and Epiphany. The Incarnation is not a matter of one day or twelve days; it is a way of life, into which we are all called. Christmas is for all year.

SCRIPTURE
The grace of God has appeared, bringing salvation to all.
                                                              Titus 2:11

MEDITATION
I have received so much by the coming of Jesus. His birth gives me hope and joy. I must not keep this good news to myself. This salvation is for all.

PRAYER
There are those, loving God, for whom Christmas is hard. They remember those they have loved and who now are dead. They have been hungry today, or the food they have had has reminded them of the hunger they face tomorrow. They have slept in the doorways, and fought to keep out the cold. Jesus knew hunger and cold, rejection and grief. Strengthen all who work to improve the lot of those who suffer, who bring justice to the world so that all may rejoice; through Jesus Christ our Lord, the Word made flesh.

A LAST PRAYER
Glory to God in the highest, and peace to people on earth.

Epiphany ✳ *Morning*

The mighty one, God the Lord, speaks and summons the earth from the rising of the sun to its setting. Out of Zion, the perfection of beauty, God shines forth.　　　　　　　*Psalm 50:1–2*

SCRIPTURE
He was revealed in flesh, vindicated in spirit,
seen by angels, proclaimed among Gentiles,
believed in through the world, taken up in glory.
　　　　　　　　　　　　　　　　　1 Timothy 3:16

MEDITATION
For Christians in the Eastern Church today is Christmas Day, whilst in the Western Church we end the Feast of Christmas. The story of the wise men reminds us that wisdom leads to worship, and that even the strangest wisdom is not rejected by God. Today we remember the beginnings of God's appearing in Jesus—at his birth, at his baptism, at the wedding where he did his first miracle.

Today I will look for Jesus in the things I begin, in my first meetings with people, and in the first words I speak.

PRAYER FOR TODAY
Teach me wisdom, Wisdom of God; teach me to worship by my way of life. At the beginning of this day, appear to me, and show me your glory in the every-day moments; through Jesus Christ our Lord.

THE LORD'S PRAYER

Epiphany ☽ *Evening*

Ascribe to the Lord the glory of his name; worship the Lord in holy splendour.
Psalm 29:2

This day was to be marked by the worship. Even where I have failed to remember this, or have worshipped someone or something other than God, God still calls me to worship now. I am silent. I adore.

SCRIPTURE

Here is my servant, whom I uphold, my chosen, in whom my soul delights; I have put my spirit on him; he will bring forth justice for the nations ... a bruised reed he will not break, and the dimly burning wick he will not quench; he will faithfully bring forth justice.
Isaiah 42:1, 3

MEDITATION

Like the grass that pushes through concrete, God persists gently but surely. The weakest are not broken, but the hardness of the world will be overcome.

PRAYER

Mary treasured your word, O God, and the wise men brought their treasures. Jesus met John in the water of the Jordan, and he turned the water of Canaan to wine. Be my treasure, and enable me to pour you out before others; be the water of life to me which becomes the wine of celebration for your world; through Jesus Christ our Lord.

A LAST PRAYER

Remember, merciful God, those who have no earthly treasure, those who have no earthly wisdom, those who hunger and thirst for your kingdom. Bring them this night the joy of your appearing.

Lent ✳ Morning

I called upon the Lord, who is worthy to be praised, so shall I be saved from my enemies.   *Psalm 18:3*

SCRIPTURE
Seek good and not evil, that you may live; and so the Lord, the God of hosts, will be with you.   *Amos 5:14*

MEDITATION
The season of Lent is an opportunity to prepare for Easter. Like an athlete I leave behind everything that hinders me in my race towards the risen Christ. In the desert Jesus decided that there was no short cut to doing God's will; the spectacular might draw attention to him, but the watchers would miss God in the excitement. Holiness comes by daily obedience.

Set yourself each day a discipline, a training schedule for meeting the risen Christ. Each day seek the good of those who experience mostly evil. Give encouragement to those who face disappointment, give hope to those who know despair. Give away something of your time, your sympathy, your self, so that out of your poverty someone else may be enriched.

PRAYER FOR TODAY
As I begin the desert road to the risen Christ, teach me to feed others as you feed me. Teach me to be a place of refreshment just as you are an oasis to me. Teach me not to hold on to what I have when you call me to empty myself to you. Keep me close to you, so that I may meet you in those who need me as I need you; through Jesus Christ our Lord.

THE LORD'S PRAYER

Lent ☽ Evening

Sing praises to the Lord, O you his faithful ones, and give thanks to his holy name. For his anger is but for a moment; his favour is for a lifetime. Weeping may linger for the night, but joy comes with the morning.   *Psalm 30:4–5*

The word of God today has been to discipline and effort. Where you have found this hard and where you have failed, there is cause for sorrow—perhaps for weeping. But this is not the end of the story. God is at work in you and in the world for joy—the joy of the creation at one with its maker and saviour.

SCRIPTURE

What does the Lord require of you but to do justice, and to love kindness, and to walk humbly with your God?   *Micah 6:8*

MEDITATION

These words were spoken to people who knew that they had to make sacrifices, but who had forgotten why. We cannot buy God off with extravagant gestures. Sacrifice reminds us that all our life is to be made holy, all our life belongs to God. Sacrifice starts in our attitudes and our daily living with other people; it reminds us of our accountability to God. The way I treat others reveals the way I think of God.

PRAYER

Deliver me from religion without love, from a believing which ignores the needs of others, from a faith which makes me arrogant; through Jesus Christ our Lord.

A LAST PRAYER

As night comes, send the dawn of your freedom on all your world. May the pain of those who sorrow be transformed by our obedience into the joy of those who have found your justice, mercy and peace.

Maundy Thursday ✳ Morning

Blessed be the name of the Lord from this time on and for ever-more.   *Psalm 113:2*

SCRIPTURE
I give you a new commandment, that you love one another. Just as I have loved you, you also should love one another.
John 13:34

MEDITATION
Today we remember how Jesus stooped to love his friends; he washed their feet—the action of a slave. He served those who would betray him, who would disown him, who would leave him in the lurch. He asks us to love one another—even those who treat us in the same shameful way.

I cannot stand on my dignity and demand privileges for myself. Today I must serve those whom I might rightfully expect to serve me. My friends and my family who wait on me hand and foot, those who should know better but who let me down—I kneel at their feet today. And not today only, for the command of Jesus is for every day.

PRAYER FOR TODAY
Teach me to love you in friend and stranger, as you have loved me when I have estranged myself from you. May your name be blessed as your love is demonstrated in lives offered to those who have nothing, who expect nothing, but who are everything to you; through Jesus Christ our Lord.

THE LORD'S PRAYER

Maundy Thursday ☾ *Evening*

As the deer longs for flowing streams; so my soul longs for you,
O God.   *Psalm 42:1*

*We need to be refreshed by God. In the hectic rush of life, we
need to pause in a quiet place, and experience once more the
purity of Jesus. Sit at the Last Supper table with Jesus, who
gives himself to you for your renewal and cleansing.*

SCRIPTURE
Come let us to up to the mountain of the Lord, to the house of
the God of Jacob; that he may teach us his ways and that we
may walk in his paths.   *Isaiah 2:3*

MEDITATION
This scripture calls us to the place where God is revealed most
clearly. For the people to whom Isaiah spoke this meant the
Temple in Jerusalem. For us it means the Cross of Christ. Here
we learn how to walk in God's way, come what may.

PRAYER
The world is your footstool, yet you wash my feet. Teach me
this night how to serve and love, as you have loved me. Bring
me to your table with all who hunger for right to prevail; bring
me to your feet with all who lie in the dust; bring me to your
Cross where you pour out your life for the world's salvation.

A LAST PRAYER
Give success, God of the water, to those who bring clean water
to the thirsty of the world. Give reward, God of the dust, to
those who serve the forgotten people. Give refreshment and
energy to those who love as you love, God of the Supper and
the Cross.

Good Friday ✳ Morning

What shall I return to the Lord for all his bounty to me? I will lift up the cup of salvation and call on the name of the Lord.

Psalm 116:12–13

SCRIPTURE

My God, my God, why have you forsaken me?   *Mark 15:34*

MEDITATION

Here is the cost of the world's salvation. Grace is free, but it is not cheap. Jesus, whose life was characterized by a sense of the closeness of God, dies feeling that God is far away. The death of Jesus is the death of all those who feel betrayed, bewildered, lost—even hopeless. When I am abandoned, when I see others rejected, my hope lies in turning to Jesus forsaken.

Make a special determination today to give away something of cost and value. Give more than you intended to a charity. Spend time with someone who will take more time than you have allowed. Allow another to have the place, the priority, that you wanted and deserved.

PRAYER FOR TODAY

Suffering God, keep me alive this day to the needs of those who feel cheated and lost. Deliver me from cheap words and empty gestures. Give me the courage to live beyond comfortable certainty, and so abandon myself to you that I may bring certain comfort to the forsaken and the destitute; through Jesus Christ our crucified Lord.

THE LORD'S PRAYER

Good Friday ☽ *Evening*

I cry aloud to God, aloud to God, that he may hear me. In the day of trouble I seek the Lord.   *Psalm 77:1–2a*

Recollect in silence those who have wept today. The dying, the bereaved, the hungry, the thirsty, the tortured, the homeless, the disappointed, the hopeless—all these have cried. Offer their tears, with the tears of Mary at the cross, to God.

SCRIPTURE
Standing near the cross of Jesus were his mother, and his mother's sister, Mary the wife of Clopas, and Mary Magdalene.
                                                                John 19:25

MEDITATION
Sometimes, I watch and I feel there is nothing I can do. I am numbed and bereft of all energy. This is the place of Mary desolate, who just stands and weeps. Her suffering is part of the Good Friday story too. When I see others who are powerless and paralysed, I turn with them and with Mary at the foot of the cross. We stand, waiting for deliverance.

PRAYER
Hear the cries of those who have lost everything and everyone they have loved. In the darkness of their sorrow, bring them the relief and the presence they seek; through Jesus Christ our crucified Lord.

A LAST PRAYER
Keep me awake a little longer tonight, dear God. Keep me watching at the foot of your cross for those whose rest is always uneasy, for those whose sleep is always disrupted, for those whose grief runs deep. Pour out a special blessing on those who sit at telephone help-lines and listen to the cries of the poor.

Holy Saturday ✳ *Morning*

Out of the depths I cry to you, O Lord. Lord, hear my voice!
Psalm 130:1–2a

SCRIPTURE

The gospel was proclaimed even to the dead, so that, though they had been judged in the flesh as everyone is judged, they might live in the spirit as God does. *1 Peter 4:6*

MEDITATION

The death of Jesus touches the whole of history. The text reminds us that beyond our death the gospel makes its way. God will not be thwarted, and the limits which confine and shackle us do not hamper the salvation which Jesus wins for the creation.

In the stillness of Holy Saturday, in the silence of the grave, listen for the gospel which death cannot muzzle or stifle. Make today an opportunity to pray for those whose special task and gift are the proclamation of the good news.

PRAYER FOR TODAY

Today the creation holds its breath, and we are waiting for your word of life from the dead. The world around me carries on its way, and I too have my cares and responsibilities. Deliver me from the dead hand of routine, and speak to the coldness of my heart and mind the word which brings release to the captive; through Jesus Christ our Lord, who dwelt among the dead for their salvation.

THE LORD'S PRAYER

Holy Saturday ☾ *Evening*

You who live in the shelter of the Most High, who abide in the shadow of the Almighty, will say to the Lord, 'My refuge and my fortress; my God, in whom I trust.'   *Psalm 91:1–2*

It is so easy to imagine that the horizon is the edge of the world. Beyond the limits of our vision, God sees. This is our ground for hope. When you despair of yourself and the world, God stands firm and brings to life what we had left for dead.

SCRIPTURE

Remember that you fashioned me like clay; and will you turn me to dust again? Did you not pour me out like milk and curdle me like cheese? You clothed me with skin and flesh, and knit me together with bone and sinews. You have granted me life and steadfast love, and your care has preserved my spirit.
                                                            Job 10:10–12

MEDITATION

God has not made me in order to destroy me. Job is a realist; he knows the awfulness of much of life. But Job is not a cynic; he knows the greatness of God. Tomorrow is the day of resurrection. Tonight is a time for vigil, for keeping watch.

PRAYER

O God, speak for the life of creation. Let the thunder of death be quelled by your mighty word. Roll back the stone of our indifference and disbelief, and release us from all that binds us and holds us back; through Jesus Christ our waiting Lord.

A LAST PRAYER

I am waiting, and I am listening. Give to your world the freedom of the children of God.

Easter Day ✳ Morning

The Lord is king! Let the earth rejoice; let the many coastlands
be glad.   *Psalm 97:1*

SCRIPTURE

Why do you look for the living among the dead? He is not here,
but has risen.   *Luke 24:5*

MEDITATION

Christ is risen, alleluia! He is risen indeed, alleluia! This is the
great Easter greeting of the Christian Church ringing
throughout its history. The worst that death can do, the utmost
destruction it can wreak, has been done. And now God has
answered the darkness of our fears, the silence of our waiting.
God has spoken, and the Word made flesh has been raised from
death. We do not understand how, but *Christ is risen, alleluia!
He is risen indeed, alleluia!*

PRAYER FOR TODAY

Speak your word of resurrection to those whose hopes are dead,
to those whose future has been stolen, to those whose lives are
empty. Gather the company of Easter people and send us out
into your world as you sent Christ. Send your Spirit of mission
upon the Church and especially on those who will be baptized
today. May the word you spoke then resound today and bring
your creation to new life and unity in you; through Jesus Christ
our risen Lord.

THE LORD'S PRAYER

Easter Day ◑ *Evening*

Come, bless the Lord, all you servants of the Lord, who stand
by night in the house of the Lord!   *Psalm 134:1*

*Think of the two disciples on the road to Emmaus, whose home
suddenly became the house of the Lord. Remember those who
live in the shanty towns and transit camps of the world. Think of
your home. Pray that the house of the Lord may be found
beyond Emmaus.*

SCRIPTURE

The hour is coming, and is now here, when the dead will hear
the voice of the Son of God, and those who hear will live.

John 5:25

MEDITATION

The world longs for life, life full to the brim. Its roads to life are
wealth and power, and they promise the bliss of escape. The
voice of the Son of God is the voice of one who did not escape,
but who entered life through death. His peace is different from
what the world offers, but it is offered to the world. And those
who hear will live. Here is the good news of Easter. It is for me,
but not for me alone. Every one who hears will live.

PRAYER

Open the ears of the deaf, open the eyes of the blind, loosen the
tongue of the dumb, that all creation may praise you for life
which death can never extinguish. Through Jesus Christ our
Lord, the first-born from the dead.

A LAST PRAYER

Shine in the darkness, and by the light of the risen Christ banish
the fears which enslave your world. Raise your creation from
the bondage of death.

Pentecost ✷ *Morning*

You make the winds your messengers, fire and flame your
ministers.   *Psalm 104:4*

SCRIPTURE
Now the Lord is the Spirit, and where the Spirit of the Lord is,
there is freedom.   *2 Corinthians 3:16*

MEDITATION
The freedom of which St Paul speaks is not freedom to act self-
ishly or without restraint. It is freedom to understand God's
purposes for the world as revealed in Jesus Christ. It is the
freedom to love, to do justice, and to serve neighbour and
stranger. Of course, Pentecost means joy and delight; but my
joy and delight are in God, the giver of every perfect gift.

*On this feast day of the Church's birth, remember how its begin-
nings were in sharing the good news of Jesus raised from the
dead. Christians must encourage and co-operate with all that is
good wherever they find it. They do so, because God is good.
What makes us different is not that we are superior, but that we
have encountered the risen Christ. God's Spirit is given to us to
enable us to live as Easter people for the salvation of the world.*

PRAYER FOR TODAY
God of freedom and of energy, root and ground your Church in
the Spirit. Make your people witnesses for you, and bring your
world speedily to its new creation; through Jesus Christ our
Lord.

THE LORD'S PRAYER

Pentecost ☽ *Evening*

Praise the Lord! Let everything that breathes praise the Lord!
Praise the Lord!   *Psalm 150:1, 6*

The Spirit who brooded over the creation is given for the life of
God's new creation. Pentecost is Easter in the lives of believers.
It is the energy source of that praise and worship which is a
world made one with God, its creator and redeemer.

SCRIPTURE
The Spirit helps us in our weakness; for we do not know how to
pray as we ought, but that very Spirit intercedes with sighs too
deep for words. And God, who searches the heart, knows what
is in the mind of the Spirit, because the Spirit intercedes for the
saints according to the will of God.   *Romans 8:26–27*

MEDITATION
This is amazing. When I do not know how to pray for myself
or for others, the Spirit of God makes sense of my prayers.
Moreover, the Spirit who indwells me understands me, and God
who sends the Spirit understands the Spirit's prayers. The circle
is complete. God's will can now be done in me and through me.
Am I ready for this?

PRAYER
I do not have the words, I do not have the vision, I cannot pray
as I should. Where my words have run out, where my vision is
dimmed or partial, speak for me, O Spirit of God; through Jesus
Christ our Lord.

A LAST PRAYER
O God of life, renew me beyond my imagining. Renew your
world beyond my dreams. Send your Spirit upon all people, and
renew the face of your creation.

INDEXES

OLD TESTAMENT READINGS

Genesis	1:31	Morning	14
	18:25	Evening	13
	32:24–26	Evening	25
Exodus	3:4b–5	Morning	5
Joshua	1:9	Morning	11
	24:15	Morning	17
Ruth	1:16	Evening	4
2 Samuel	22:29	Evening	31
Nehemiah	8:10	Morning	3
Job	2:13	Evening	30
	10:10–12	Evening	Holy Saturday
Proverbs	3:5–6	Morning	9
	3:11–12	Evening	17
	22:22–23	Morning	27
Ecclesiastes	8:1	Morning	24
Isaiah	2:3	Evening	Maundy Thursday
	26:3	Morning	7
	26:4	Morning	12
	30:15	Evening	2
	42:1, 3	Evening	Epiphany
	43:1c–3a	Morning	16
	43:25	Evening	9
	44:22	Evening	22
	46:4	Evening	15
	55:12	Morning	1
Jeremiah	17:14	Evening	23
	29:7	Morning	8
	29:13–14a	Morning	15
	31:3	Evening	7
Lamentations	3:22–23	Morning	22
Ezekiel	36:26	Evening	12
	37:14	Evening	29
Hosea	6:1	Evening	18
	14:5,7	Evening	20
Amos	5:14	Morning	Lent
Micah	6:8	Evening	Lent
Habakkuk	3:18	Morning	18
Zechariah	2:5	Evening	3
	3:4b	Evening	1
Malachi	3:7	Evening	8

NEW TESTAMENT READINGS

Matthew	5:6, 9	Morning	4
	5:16	Morning	30
	6:21	Morning	26
	11:28	Evening	10
	13:45–46	Morning	19
	18:1–3	Morning	25
	25:40	Evening	19
Mark	4:26–27, 29	Evening	Advent
	5:34	Evening	24
	10:44–45	Morning	20
	15:34	Morning	Good Friday
Luke	11:28	Morning	13
	13:20	Morning	31
	15:7	Evening	26
	24:5	Morning	Easter Day
John	1:1, 14	Morning	Christmas
	1:43	Morning	10
	4:14	Evening	6
	5:25	Evening	Easter Day
	8:12	Morning	21
	13:34	Morning	Maundy Thursday
	19:25	Evening	Good Friday
	20:23	Evening	21
Romans	5:6	Evening	11
	8:26–27	Evening	Pentecost
	12:9	Morning	6
2 Corinthians	3:3	Morning	23
	3:16	Morning	Pentecost
	4:8–10	Evening	14
	12:9	Morning	29
Ephesians	5:14b	Morning	Advent
Philippians	1:6	Evening	28
	3:13–14	Evening	27
	4:8	Morning	2
1 Timothy	1:15	Evening	5
	3:16	Morning	Epiphany
Titus	2:11	Evening	Christmas
Hebrews	11:22–24a	Morning	Sunday
1 Peter	2:10	Evening	16
	4:6	Morning	Holy Saturday
Revelation	3:8	Morning	28
	4:8b	Evening	Sunday

PSALTER INDEX

80:3	Evening	7
80:7	Evening	21
81:1	Morning	31
84:1	Evening	Sunday
85:11	Evening	Advent
86:15	Evening	13
88:1–2	Evening	10
89:6	Morning	23
90:1–2	Evening	Holy Saturday
93:1	Morning	28
95:6	Morning	14
96:1	Morning	6
97:1	Morning	Easter Day
98:1, 4a	Morning	Christmas
100:1–2	Morning	27
103:8	Evening	9
103:12	Evening	29
104:1–2	Morning	7
104:4	Morning	Pentecost
104:24	Morning	30
107:1	Morning	11
108:4	Morning	25
109:26	Evening	8
113:2	Morning	Maundy Thursday
113:3	Morning	15
116:7	Evening	28
116:12–13	Morning	Good Friday
118:1	Morning	20
118:5	Evening	14
118:24	Morning	1
119:105	Morning	16
121:1–2	Morning	10
123:2	Evening	4
124:8	Evening	18
130:1–2a	Morning	Holy Saturday
134:1	Evening	Easter Day
136:3	Evening	24
139:11–12	Evening	2
145:3	Morning	24
147:1	Morning	12
149:1	Morning	Sunday
150:1, 6	Evening	Pentecost

About the Joint Liturgical Group of Great Britain

A short history

The Joint Liturgical Group [JLG] began in 1963. Its aim has always been to serve the churches of Britain in the renewal of their worship. It was registered in law as a trust in 1971. JLG has been concerned with the demands of worship in Britain, and the development of common liturgical thinking and texts in the worldwide Church.

Members of the JLG were part of ICET (International Consultation on English Texts, 1969–1974), and helped to prepare the texts published as *Prayers we have in Common* (1970, 1971, 1975). Since 1985 JLG has been a member of ELLC (English Language Liturgical Consultation), which in 1988 agreed the texts published as *Praying Together* (Canterbury Press, 1990).

JLG's particular vocation relates to English-language worship within the churches in England, Scotland and Wales.

Purposes

JLG exists –

- to be a creative working group. It offers rites and texts to the churches and ecumenical bodies, and advises and comments on worship matters. Work produced by JLG is offered to churches to use as they see fit.
- to act for the churches, or for groups of churches, where this is useful and appropriate.
- to join with ELLC and other international bodies concerned with English-language worship.
- to serve the liturgical needs of congregations linked with more than one British church.
- to liaise with bodies and officers who have responsibility in different churches for worship matters. JLG assists in the exchange of liturgical news between the churches.

Present and future

JLG and its work are formally recognized by the Council of Churches for Britain and Ireland.

JLG affirms its relationship to the developing life of the churches, and continues to be willing to serve them in the God-given calling of praise and witness.